Effortless Mediterranean Diet Slow Cooker Cookbook

Easy Everyday Slow Cooker Mediterranean Recipes for a Healthy Lifestyle

Madison Miller

Copyrights

All rights reserved © 2018 by Madison Miller and The Cookbook Publisher. No part of this publication or the information in it may be quoted from or reproduced in any form by means such as printing, scanning, photocopying, or otherwise without prior written permission of the copyright holder.

Disclaimer and Terms of Use

This book is presented solely for motivational and informational purposes. The author and the publisher do not hold any responsibility for errors, omissions, or contrary interpretation of the subject matter herein. The recipes provided in this book are for informational purposes only and are not intended to provide dietary advice. A medical practitioner should be consulted before making any changes in diet. Additionally, recipes' cooking times may require adjustment depending on age and quality of appliances. Readers are strongly urged to take all precautions to ensure ingredients are fully cooked to avoid the dangers of foodborne illnesses. The recipes and suggestions provided in this book are solely the opinions of the author. The author and publisher do not take any responsibility for any consequences that may result due to following the instructions provided in this book. All the nutritional information contained in this book is provided for informational purposes only. This information is based on the specific brands, ingredients, and measurements used to make the recipe and therefore the nutritional information is an estimate, and in no way is intended to be a guarantee of the actual nutritional value of the recipe made in the reader's home. The author and the publisher will not be responsible for any damages resulting in your reliance on the nutritional information.

ISBN: 9781724056696

Printed in the United States

Contents

Introduction _____ 1

About the Mediterranean Diet _____ 2

Cooking with a Slow Cooker _____ 6

Breakfast Recipes _____ 13

Poultry Recipes _____ 21

Beef and Veal Recipes _____ 33

Pork and Lamb Recipes _____ 47

Fish and Seafood Recipes _____ 57

Vegetarian Recipes _____ 65

Soup Recipes _____ 75

Desserts _____ 81

Recipe Index _____ 89

Also by Madison Miller _____ 91

Cooking Conversion Charts _____ 93

Introduction

The slow cooker is probably one of the greatest culinary inventions of modern times. It not only allows you the freedom to go about your day without having to worry about preparing a meal; the slow cooking process makes meat more succulent and infuses your meals with bursts of flavor that can be achieved in no other way. Many people associate slow cookers with rich stews and hearty roasts, but they can also prepare food for other diets—and the Mediterranean diet is one that benefits greatly from the use of a slow cooker.

The Mediterranean diet is a heart-healthy diet that eliminates added sugars, trans fat, refined grains and oils, processed meat and all highly processed food products, and a slow cooker doesn't require added oils, processed meats or refined grains to create amazing, delicious, healthy meals. Although many of these recipes may have some flour or a few other extras, they are still much healthier than standard North American cuisine.

The Mediterranean diet is known to contribute to the improvement of overall health and decreased incidences of cancer and high blood pressure. The whole grains used in the recipes from this region contain few unhealthy fats, while the liberal use of nuts, avocados, salmon and tuna supplies plenty of healthy fats.

The recipes in this book show you how to use your slow cooker to prepare heart-healthy Mediterranean meals for breakfast, lunch, dinner and even dessert. Snacks, appetizers, and sides are not neglected either. You'll be able to enjoy a wonderful slow-cooked side dish with a fillet of salmon-rich in omega-3 fatty acid, or toss ingredients into the slow cooker at night and wake up to warm, tasty meal to start your day. From oatmeal to tiramisu bread pudding, the recipes in this book are sure to please.

About the Mediterranean Diet

An extraordinary number of people spend an inordinate amount of time trying diet after diet with the single goal of losing weight. The unfortunate reality, however, is that despite various levels of initial success, the weight returns with a vengeance simply because once the weight is gone, people revert to their pre-diet lifestyles. The Mediterranean diet is a healthy alternative that promotes a long-term lifestyle change. This change is relatively simple and exquisitely pain-free because there are very few foods you have to sacrifice to sustain your new healthy eating habits.

The Mediterranean diet is a heart-healthy diet that emphasizes the elimination of added sugars, trans fat, refined grains and oils, processed meat and all highly processed food products. What you get in return are flavorful olive oils, spicy nuts, fish and chicken, a sprinkling of red meat, vegetables, whole grains (including bread and pasta), and enough herbs and spices to enhance your food and make your taste buds sing and your nose dance right along. The Mediterranean diet even allows for a glass of red wine every evening if you so choose. This diet is not a diet per se that restrict your from eating but it's a LIFESTYLE that focuses on healthier habits. It includes mainly changes in the way nourish our body and being active every day.

The Mediterranean diet combines cuisines from Greece, Italy, and Spain, emphasizing the foods from each of these nations which provide the most health benefits. One of the main components of the diet is olive oil. Studies have suggested that olive oil decreases the incidence of cancer, heart issues, stroke, and other illnesses. Improvement of overall health and lower blood pressure are additional benefits of the Mediterranean diet. The whole grains used in the recipes from this region contain healthy nutrients and are fulfilling. Nuts and avocados are used freely because they are excellent sources of healthy fats, as are the salmon and tuna you find in many Mediterranean recipes.

The recipes in this book are just a sample of the many choices available to you on the Mediterranean diet. You will appreciate the fact that you will never be hungry on this plan, as this book provides a collection of healthy recipes for breakfast, lunch, and dinner, as well as appetizers, snacks, side dishes, and yes, even dessert. After completing the week of recipes found herein, you will be one step closer to achieving such a healthy and flavorful change that you will hardly notice nor remember what you gave up.

For more than fifty years, the scientific data accumulated relative to the Mediterranean diet have shown that following a healthy lifestyle that focuses on the Mediterranean diet have shown that it reduces the risks of heart attacks, strokes, and other heart illnesses, as well as diabetes, cancer, Alzheimer's type dementia, and even depression. These health benefit in itself should be enough to motivate anyone to give it a try.

The Principles of the Mediterranean diet

There are seven main principles at the foundation of the Mediterranean diet. These are often represented in the food pyramid below for a quick and easy visual impact. The principles include:

1. Foods that are consumed most often, but not exclusively, are of plant origin, particularly: whole grains and whole grain cereals, vegetables, legumes (beans, lentils, peas, and peanuts), and fruits.

2. Animal products like red meats should be consumed in a moderate way (principle of frugality), just a few times a month.

3. The food consumed is very varied (principle of diversity) and produced locally (principle of local supply). A varied diet is always more enjoyable than eating the same every day. If you eat local produce and other local ingredients, it will contain more nutrients your body needs to thrive and you contribute to the local economy.

4. The produces are consumed according to the seasonal cycle (seasonality principle). The fresher a produce is, the more nutritious it is and eating according to the season will make you healthier.

5. The consumption of sweet products is limited and reserved for holidays (principle of frugality). Healthy sweets can be consumed a few times a month. Avoid all processed foods, especially those containing refined sugar in all its forms such as corn syrup, fructose, sucrose, etc.

6. Olive oil is consumed in the usual way for seasoning and cooking on a daily basis. If you can opt for the extra virgin olive oil first cold pressed. You can also use other healthy fats such as avocados, sunflower oil, and grapeseed oil. Avoid butter and choose one of these healthier alternatives.

7. To enhance the taste of food, instead of salt, we use herbs and spices, as well as onion and garlic. Your arteries will thank you and will remain healthy!

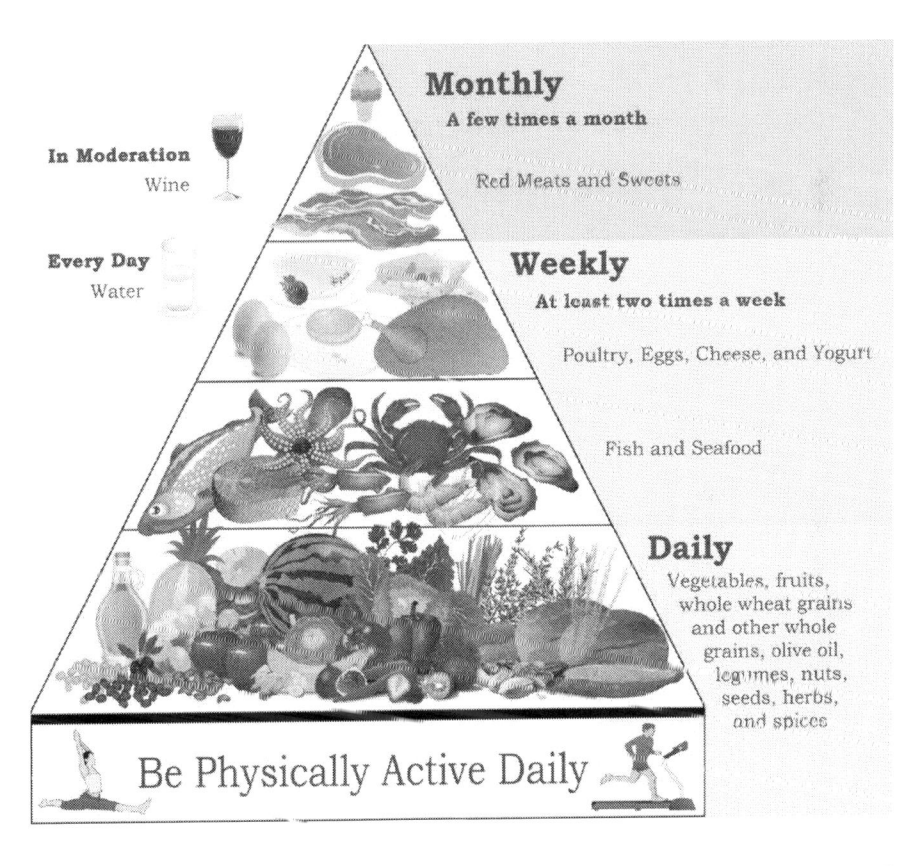

Monthly
A few times a month
Red Meats and Sweets

In Moderation
Wine

Every Day
Water

Weekly
At least two times a week
Poultry, Eggs, Cheese, and Yogurt

Fish and Seafood

Daily
Vegetables, fruits, whole wheat grains and other whole grains, olive oil, legumes, nuts, seeds, herbs, and spices

Be Physically Active Daily

All the recipes in this cookbook are based on these principles of the Mediterranean diet. I invite you to try them because, in addition to being a real asset to your health, they are easy to prepare and especially delicious.

Cooking with a Slow Cooker

You might be interested to hear that the idea of the slow cooker goes back to the 1930s when a man named Irving Naxon developed a similar pot, which he designed to provide a steady source of low heat to a pot of beans. His mother was from Lithuania and her family was Jewish; they did not cook on Saturdays because they were observing the Sabbath. They used to make a bean stew called *cholent*, which would go into the pot on Friday night, and then cook all day to be ready to eat after services on Saturday evening. This was his inspiration for the invention.

He sold his design in the 1970s to a company that used it to make the first Crock Pot. The advent of the microwave slowed the device's popularity for a while, but they are still going strong today, and Crock Pot is no longer the only brand. Manufacturers who make similar appliances refer to theirs as *slow cookers* for trademark reasons, but you can use them all the same way.

There are some things to know when you are shopping for a slow cooker. Features vary a little, and so do the sizes.

Most slow cookers have a LOW and HIGH setting, and this is important for most recipes because it tells you how long to cook the food. Others have a KEEP WARM option, which is good if the food is ready before you are. Timers are helpful too, and don't assume that the less expensive models will have this feature – some don't. If you want to be able to set it and have it turn off while you're out, you'll need the timer.

Keep in mind the size of your family and what kind of dishes you would like to prepare in the slow cooker. Large pots, 4- and 6-

quart, are good for large roasts, whole chickens, and stews. They're the most useful slow cookers, but if a recipe is too small it will spread out too much, and your meal will be overcooked. For things like side dishes, desserts, warm dips, and to feed two people, choose a 2-quart slow cooker. It's good to have more than one to choose from.

Tips for Using Slow Cookers

Knowing how to best use a slow cooker can really be a game changer in terms of simplifying your life. Here are a few tips that can make using your slow cooker an even more satisfying experience.

1. Meal plan and pre-prep your food as much as possible. It is true that sometimes you can just throw random ingredients into a slow cooker and turn out a masterpiece. It is also true that sometimes that philosophy can result in a culinary disaster. I know that you are probably busy, and meal planning may or may not be something that is on your priority list. However, you should at least try to give a little thought to what you might like to cook during the week. Taking a little time at the beginning of the week can actually save you big time over the course of the week. Also, if you know you are going to be preparing a certain dish or using specific ingredients, pre-wash or cut them in advance to save yourself sometime later. This is especially helpful if you are assembling a slow cooker full of goodness in the morning before you rush out the door.

2. To really make your slow cooker meal a no-fuss event, prepare everything the night before. You can brown meat, cut vegetables, and assemble everything in the evening.

Once it is assembled, place it in the refrigerator and simply grab it and get it going in the morning.

3. In most cases, slow cooker times can be adjusted to suit your schedule. If you would like to shorten the cooking time, simply cut back a little on the ingredients and increase the temperature to high. Generally speaking, increasing the temperature can take two to four hours off the cooking time, depending on the dish.

4. Consider browning the meat. Many of the recipes in this book call for browning the meat, or quickly sautéing some vegetables. Do you really need to do this step? For that question, the answer is no. However, if you are looking for the highest quality results, then do it. Browning the meat before you place it in the slow cooker helps to maintain the moisture, flavor, and juiciness of the meat. When you sauté vegetables, you change the character of the ingredient and alter the flavor slightly, to something a little more desirable. Take onions, for instance. You can just place them in the slow cooker. They will absorb juices and soften during cooking. The result is often delicious. Other times, you might want to sauté them a little to bring out their natural sweetness to a level that slow cooking alone is unable to do.

5. When you brown your meat, don't forget to scrape the pan. There is an awful lot of goodness left in the bottom of a pan that a piece of meat has been browned in. The same is true for the oils or moisture left after sautéing vegetables. Take the extra minute and scrape the pan into the slow cooker to keep all the extra flavor.

6. Beware the dairy. If you are following a ketogenic diet, you are likely also enjoying creamy, full-fat dairy products

daily. Full-fat dairy is great as it provides valuable nutrition and important fat calories. You can include full-fat dairy in your slow cooker creations, you just have to be a little thoughtful of how you do it. First of all, dairy that sits in the heat all day is going to curdle a bit. This is fine if it is a small amount and it is mixed with other ingredients to help offset the effect. Sometimes the thickening that happens is just what you are looking for. However, in most cases when you are using larger amounts of dairy, you will want to add it towards the end of the cooking time, usually in the last hour of cooking. This will help maintain the texture and integrity of the dairy ingredients. It adds a little bit of time at the end, but it is well worth it.

7. Use the highest quality ingredients you can afford. Many times, when someone has a negative slow cooker experience, it is because they used inferior ingredients. This doesn't mean you have to break the bank on all grass-fed or organic ingredients. What it does mean is pay attention to where your money is best spent on quality, and where you can afford to skimp. Also, cook with ingredients that are in season in your area whenever possible. A tomato that comes from the farmer across town is going to be far superior to one that traveled a thousand miles just to reach your grocer's shelf.

8. Don't overfill your slow cooker. For best results, your slow cooker should not be more than three-quarters full. This allows plenty of room for the heat to circulate and cook everything evenly. If you find that your slow cooker is overstuffed, simply cut back on the bulky ingredients a little, or use a larger pot.

9. Resist the temptation to constantly be lifting the lid and inhaling the savory aroma. Yes, it smells great. However, you are disrupting the cooking process by allowing the heat to escape. The slow cooker then has to work to get back up to the proper cooking temperature again, and your food will take extra time to cook.

10. Consider the placement of the ingredients in your slow cooker. One of the best features of a slow cooker is the "dump and go" potential. Slow cooker meals are generally low fuss and require little more than just tossing the ingredients in and turning it on. There are times, though, when a little forethought about how the ingredients are placed can make a big difference to the end result. The most heat is going to come from the bottom of the device. This means that what you put on the bottom is going to have more surface-to-surface heat. Sometimes, you might want this to be the meat. Other times, you might want this to be vegetables or liquids. For example, a layer of onions under a roast lifts the meat up just enough to allow more even cooking throughout while also leaving the onions nice and tender and in a position to absorb all of the delicious juices during cooking.

11. Cut your ingredients in uniform pieces and keep texture in mind. Raw pumpkin is quite dense and can be cut into smaller, even pieces to ensure they are cooked to tender perfection. Mushrooms, on the other hand, cook quite

quickly and should be added in large pieces, or even in the last hour or two of cooking, if you will be home to add them. Spinach and other greens should be added a short while before serving, when this is possible, to give them time to wilt.

12. The meat thermometer is your friend. Even if that roast has been in there for eight hours and it looks delectably done, take a minute and stick a meat thermometer in it. For most meats that are not beef, you want a temperature of 160°F. With beef, you can have a bit more of a range depending upon the doneness you prefer. As a reference, 140°F is considered medium rare for beef.

13. Your slow cooker not only makes leftovers super easy, but they often taste even better. The slow cooking process gives the ingredients more time together to build up the flavor. If you have leftovers, simply refrigerate them overnight and turn the slow cooker back on the next day. Add a little extra liquid if you need to for moisture.

Caring for Your Slow Cooker

Your slow cooker's instruction manual contains the most pertinent information for caring for your slow cooker. Here are some basic tips:

- Try not to cook longer than the cooking time given in the recipe so the food doesn't get burned.
- Do not add cold ingredients to a slow cooker that has already been heated. The insert is sensitive and may crack or break.
- Turn off, unplug, and allow your slow cooker to cool down before cleaning.
- The heating base should not be submerged in water or any liquid.
- Always remove the lid first before removing the insert or stoneware.
- The slow cooker insert is dishwasher safe. When using the dishwasher isn't enough, the following may be used:
    - hot, soapy water
    - baking soda (for gentle scrubbing)
    - vinegar
- Use a slow cooker liner or non-stick cooking spray for easy cleaning after cooking.

Remember these simple tips and you'll be able to use your slow cooker for many meals and through many happy family occasions!

Now with all this information, you are now ready to prepare delicious Slow Cooker Mediterranean meals your friends and family will enjoy. Let's start cooking!

Breakfast Recipes

Egg and Vegetable Breakfast Casserole

Breakfast is oftentimes overlooked as a slow cooker meal. But this breakfast casserole is well worth taking the time to put together the night before. You can wake up a little early to reheat it, or just set the timer so it's ready when the family wakes up. Chock full of vegetables and protein, this casserole is a great way to start your day.

Serves 8 | Prep. time 15 minutes | Cooking time 4 hours

Ingredients
8 eggs
4 egg whites
¾ cup milk (can use almond)
2 teaspoons stone ground mustard
½ teaspoon garlic salt
1 teaspoon salt
½ teaspoon pepper
1 30-ounce bag frozen hash browns
4 strips cooked bacon (optional)
½ onion, roughly chopped
2 bell peppers, roughly chopped
1 small head of broccoli, roughly chopped
6 ounces cheddar cheese

Directions
1. Mix together the eggs, egg whites, milk, mustard, garlic salt, salt, and pepper until well combined.
2. Spray the inside of the slow cooker with olive oil.
3. Spread half of the bag of hash browns across the bottom of the slow cooker and then top with bacon.

4. Pour egg mixture over the bacon and potatoes.
5. Add the onion, bell peppers and broccoli, then top with remaining hash browns and cheese.
6. Cook on low for 4 hours.

Nutrition (per serving)
Calories 320, fat 13 g, carbs 29 g,
protein 22 g, sodium 700 mg

Breakfast Stuffed Peppers

These stuffed peppers are a delicious spin on the traditional recipe. The vitamins and minerals in the peppers combined with the protein in the eggs and sausage make it a healthy and delicious beginning to any day. The beautiful presentation also makes for a special breakfast to serve to guests.

Serves 4 | Prep. time 10 minutes | Cooking time 2–4 hours

Ingredients
½ pound ground breakfast sausage
4 bell peppers (any color—I like to use one of each)
6 large eggs
4 ounces Monterey Jack Cheese, shredded
4 ounces fire-roasted chopped green chilies
¼ teaspoon salt
⅛ teaspoon pepper

Directions
1. Wash the peppers, cut off the tops and clean out the seeds.
2. Brown the sausage in a skillet. You can use turkey or chicken sausage too, but you need to add a tablespoon of oil to the pan if you do.
3. In a mixing bowl, whisk your eggs until fluffy. Then mix in the cheese and green chilies.
4. Season the egg mixture with salt and pepper.
5. Spray the slow cooker with olive oil and place the peppers inside.
6. Fill each pepper to the top with the egg mixture.
7. Set the slow cooker to high and cook for 2 hours, or cook on low for 4 hours.
8. Serve when egg mixture is set.

Nutrition (per serving)
Calories 261, fat 16.8 g, carbs 9.2 g,
protein 17.3 g, sodium 401 mg

Slow Cooker Frittata

This tasty frittata is super easy to prepare in the slow cooker. The creamy eggs and salty bite of the feta cheese complement the perfectly cooked vegetables.

Serves 6 | Prep. time 30 minutes | Cooking time 2 hours

Ingredients
1 (14-ounce) can small artichoke hearts, drained and cut into bite-sized pieces
1 (12-ounce) jar roasted red peppers, drained and cut into bite-sized pieces
¼ cup sliced green onions
8 eggs, beaten
4 ounces crumbled Feta cheese
1 teaspoon seasoning salt
½ teaspoon pepper
¼ cup chopped cilantro

Directions
1. Spray the slow cooker with olive oil and add the artichoke hearts, red peppers, and green onions.
2. Pour the beaten eggs over the top of the vegetables and stir to combine.
3. Season the mixture with pepper and seasoning salt.
4. Mix in the chopped cilantro.
5. Top with Feta cheese.
6. Cook on low for 2–3 hours or until set.

Nutrition (per serving)
Calories 243, fat 14.5 g, carbs 12.7g,
protein 15.4 g, sodium 364 mg

Cranberry Apple Oatmeal

This healthy oatmeal is packed full of autumn flavors. It's easy to prepare and tastes amazing.

Serves 4 | Prep. time 5 minutes | Cooking time 3–6 hours

Ingredients
4 cups water
2 cups old-fashioned oats
½ cup dried cranberries
2 apples, peeled and diced
¼ cup brown sugar
2 tablespoons butter, melted
½ teaspoon salt
1 teaspoon cinnamon

Directions
1. Spray your slow cooker with nonstick cooking spray.
2. Add all of the ingredients to the slow cooker and stir to combine.
3. Cook on low for 3 hours. If you want to prepare this the night before, you can cook it up to 6 hours or so. The consistency of the oats will be different if cooked overnight, but it will still be delicious

Nutrition (per serving)
Calories 254, fat 7.2 g, carbs 40.9 g, protein 6.4 g, sodium 138 mg

Blueberry Banana Steel Cut Oats

This is another quick and easy overnight oatmeal recipe that is sure to please the whole family. You can make enough on Sunday to last for a couple of days of breakfasts. It is a tasty, healthy way to start your day.

Serves 4 | Prep. time 5 minutes | Cooking time 5–8 hours

Ingredients
1 cup steel cut oats
2 ripe bananas, sliced or mashed
1–2 cups fresh or frozen blueberries
2 cups water
2 cups milk (almond milk works very well in this recipe)
2 tablespoons honey or pure maple syrup
¼ teaspoon salt
1 teaspoon cinnamon
2 teaspoons vanilla
Optional add-ins: chopped nuts, nut butter, fresh or dried fruit, granola, shredded coconut, honey, additional milk

Directions
1. Spray your slow cooker with nonstick cooking spray.
2. Add all the ingredients to the slow cooker and mix well.
3. Cook on low overnight for 6–8 hours or cook on high for 2–3 hours.

Nutrition (per serving)
Calories 297, fat 4.4 g, carbs 58 g,
protein 8 g, sodium 81 mg

Berry Breakfast Quinoa

Quinoa is a healthy and delicious alternative to oatmeal. Quinoa provides a vast amount of health benefits and its texture offers a tasty bite. The avocado adds a smooth texture and healthy fats.

Serves 8 | Prep. time 5 minutes | Cook time 2–3 hours

Ingredients
1 large avocado, pitted and smashed (you can replace with bananas)
4 cups water
2 cups quinoa, rinsed
2 cups fresh or frozen mixed berries (any fruit will work well in this recipe)
2 tablespoons pure maple syrup
2 teaspoons vanilla
1 teaspoon cinnamon
¼ teaspoon salt

Directions
1. Spray your slow cooker with nonstick cooking spray.
2. Add all the ingredients to the slow cooker and mix well.
3. Cook on low for 5 hours or high for 2–3 hours.

Nutrition (per serving)
Calories 229, fat 2.8 g, carbs 44 g,
protein 7 g, sodium 90 mg

Poultry Recipes

Slow Cooker Greek Chicken

This aromatic, flavor-packed chicken recipe will make everyone in the house salivate in anticipation. Herbs, spices and Kalamata olives make this dish a mouthwatering treat for your taste buds.

Serves 4 | Prep. time 20 minutes | Cooking time 3 hours

Ingredients
1 tablespoon extra-virgin olive oil
2 pounds boneless, skinless chicken breasts or thighs
½ teaspoon kosher salt
¼ teaspoon ground black pepper
1 (12-ounce) jar roasted red peppers, drained and chopped
1 cup Kalamata olives
1 medium red onion, cut into chunks
3 tablespoons red wine vinegar
1 tablespoon minced garlic (from about 3 large cloves)
1 teaspoon honey
1 teaspoon dried oregano
1 teaspoon dried thyme
½ cup feta cheese (optional, for serving)
Chopped fresh herbs: any mix of basil, parsley, or thyme (optional, for serving)

Directions
1. Spray your slow cooker with nonstick cooking spray or olive oil.
2. Heat the olive oil in a large skillet.
3. Season each side of the chicken breasts with salt and pepper.

4. When the oil is hot, add the chicken breasts and sear on both sides (about 3 minutes).
5. After the chicken is browned, transfer it to the slow cooker.
6. Add the red peppers, olives, and red onion to the chicken breasts. Try to place the vegetables around the chicken and not directly on top.
7. In a small bowl, mix together the vinegar, garlic, honey, oregano, and thyme. When it is well combined, pour it over the chicken.
8. Cook the chicken on low for 3 hours or until no longer pink in the middle.
9. Serve with crumbled feta cheese and fresh herbs.

Nutrition (per serving)
Calories 399, fat 17 g, carbs 13g,
protein 50 g, sodium 1093 mg

Chicken Gyros

These chicken gyros are full of flavor and spice. Healthy vegetables, herbs, and spices combine to create the perfect lunch or dinner.

Serves 4 | Prep. time 10 minutes | Cook time 3–4 hours

Ingredients
2 pounds boneless skinless chicken breasts or chicken tenders
Juice of one lemon
3 cloves garlic
2 teaspoons red wine vinegar
2–3 tablespoons olive oil
½ cup Greek yogurt
2 teaspoons dried oregano
2–4 teaspoons Greek seasoning
½ small red onion, chopped
2 tablespoons dill weed

Tzatziki Sauce
1 cup plain Greek yogurt
1 tablespoon dill weed
1 small English cucumber, chopped
Pinch of salt and pepper
1 teaspoon onion powder

Toppings: tomatoes, chopped cucumbers, chopped red onion, diced feta cheese, crumbled pita bread

Directions
1. Cut the chicken breasts into cubes and place in the slow cooker.
2. Add the lemon juice, garlic, vinegar, olive oil, Greek yogurt, oregano, Greek seasoning, red onion, and dill to the slow cooker and stir to make sure everything is well combined.
3. Cook on low for 5–6 hours or on high for 2–3 hours.
4. While the chicken is cooking, combine all ingredients for the tzatziki sauce and stir. When well mixed, put in the refrigerator until the chicken is done.
5. When the chicken has finished cooking, serve with pita bread and any or all of the toppings listed above.

Nutrition (per serving)
Calories 317, fat 7.4 g, carbs 36.1 g,
protein 28.6 g, sodium 324 mg

Slow Cooker Chicken Cassoulet

This rich, aromatic slow-cooked cassoulet is a traditional French dish. This almost soup-like stew is delicious served with a nice crusty French bread.

Serves 16 | Prep. time 10 minutes | Cooking time 20 minutes

Ingredients
1 cup dry navy beans, soaked (you can use any kind of canned bean as well)
8 bone-in skinless chicken thighs
1 Polish sausage, cooked and chopped into bite-sized pieces (optional)
1¼ cup tomato juice
1 (28-ounce) can halved tomatoes
1 tablespoon Worcestershire sauce
1 teaspoon instant beef or chicken bouillon granules
½ teaspoon dried basil
½ teaspoon dried oregano
½ teaspoon paprika
½ cup chopped celery
½ cup chopped carrot
½ cup chopped onion

Directions
1. Spray the slow cooker with olive oil or nonstick cooking spray
2. In a mixing bowl, stir together the tomato juice, tomatoes, Worcestershire sauce, beef bouillon, basil, oregano, and paprika. Make sure the ingredients are well combined.
3. Place the chicken and sausage into the slow cooker and cover with the tomato juice mixture. Top with celery, carrot, and onion.
4. Cook on low for 10–12 hours or on high for 5–6 hours.

Nutrition (per serving)
Calories 244, fat 7 g, carbs 25 g,
protein 21 g, sodium 405 mg

Slow Cooker Chicken Provencal

These Provencal chicken breasts are loaded with protein and are a delicious lunch choice. The herbs and spices marry with the chicken and beans to create an amazing flavor.

Serves 4 | Prep. time 5 minutes | Cooking time 8 hours

Ingredients
4 (6-ounce) skinless bone-in chicken breast halves
2 teaspoons dried basil
1 teaspoon dried thyme
⅛ teaspoon salt
⅛ teaspoon freshly ground black pepper
1 yellow pepper, diced
1 red pepper, diced
1 (15.5-ounce) can cannellini beans, rinsed and drained
1 (14.5-ounce) can petite diced tomatoes with basil, garlic, and oregano, undrained

Directions
1. Spray the slow cooker with nonstick cooking spray or olive oil.
2. Add all the ingredients to the slow cooker and stir to combine.
3. Cook on low for 8 hours.

Nutrition (per serving)
Calories 304, fat 4.5 g, carbs 27.3 g,
protein 39.4 g, sodium 718 mg

Greek Style Turkey Roast

This turkey roast recipe makes for an elegant meal to serve family or guests. It is rich in flavor and smells divine.

Serves 8 | Prep. time 20 minutes | Cook time 7½ hours

Ingredients
1 (4-pound) boneless turkey breast, trimmed
½ cup chicken broth, divided
2 tablespoons fresh lemon juice
2 cups chopped onion
½ cup pitted Kalamata olives
½ cup oil-packed sun-dried tomatoes, thinly sliced
1 teaspoon Greek seasoning
½ teaspoon salt
¼ teaspoon fresh ground black pepper
3 tablespoons all-purpose flour (or whole wheat)

Directions
1. Spray the slow cooker with nonstick cooking spray or olive oil.
2. Add the turkey, ¼ cup of the chicken broth, lemon juice, onion, olives, sun-dried tomatoes, Greek seasoning, salt and pepper to the slow cooker.
3. Cook on low for 7 hours.
4. Whisk the flour into the remaining ¼ cup of chicken broth, then stir gently into the slow cooker.
5. Cook for an additional 30 minutes.

Nutrition (per serving)
Calories 341, fat 19 g, carbs 6.1 g,
protein 36.4 g, sodium 465 mg

Garlic Chicken with Couscous

This simple chicken dinner is easy to prepare but makes a flavorful and satisfying meal, especially on a cold evening.

Serves 4 | Prep. time 25 minutes | Cooking time 4–7 hours

Ingredients
1 whole chicken, cut into pieces
1 tablespoon extra-virgin olive oil
6 cloves garlic, halved
1 cup dry white wine
1 cup couscous
½ teaspoon salt
½ teaspoon pepper
1 medium onion, thinly sliced
2 teaspoons dried thyme
⅓ cup whole wheat flour

Directions
1. Heat the olive oil in a heavy skillet. When skillet is hot, add the chicken to sear. Make sure the chicken pieces don't touch each other. Cook with the skin side down for about 3 minutes or until browned.
2. Spray your slow cooker with nonstick cooking spray or olive oil.
3. Put the onion, garlic, and thyme into the slow cooker and sprinkle with salt and pepper.
4. Add the chicken on top of the onions.
5. In a separate bowl, whisk the flour into the wine until there are no lumps, then pour over the chicken.
6. Cook the chicken on low for 7 hours or until done. You can cook on high for 3 hours as well.
7. Serve the chicken over the cooked couscous and spoon sauce over the top.

Nutrition (per serving)
Calories 440, fat 17.5 g, carbs 34.7 g,
protein 35.8 g, sodium 359 mg

Chicken Karahi

This curry dish is nothing less than a flavor explosion. The perfect dish to warm you up on a cold winter's night!

Serves 4 | Prep. time 5 minutes | Cooking time 4–5 hours

Ingredients
2 pounds chicken breasts or thighs, cut into bite-sized pieces
¼ cup olive oil
1 small can tomato paste
1 tablespoon butter
1 large onion, diced
½ cup plain Greek yogurt
½ cup water
2 tablespoons ginger in garlic paste (you'll find it in the produce section of your grocery store)
3 tablespoons fenugreek leaves
1 teaspoon ground coriander
1 medium tomato
1 teaspoon red chili
2 green chilies
1 teaspoon turmeric
1 tablespoon garam masala
1 teaspoon cumin powder
1 teaspoon sea salt
¼ teaspoon nutmeg

Directions
1. Spray the slow cooker with nonstick cooking spray.
2. In a small bowl, thoroughly mix together all of the spices.
3. Add the chicken to the slow cooker followed by the rest of the ingredients, including the spice mixture. Stir until everything is well mixed with the spices.

4. Cook on low for 4–5 hours.
5. Serve with naan or Italian bread.

Nutrition (per serving)
Calories 345, fat 9.9 g, carbs 8.2 g,
protein 53.7 g, sodium 364 mg

Chicken Cacciatore with Orzo

This easy slow cooker recipe will taste like you spent hours slaving over the stove. The pasta cooks in the pot with the chicken, so it is literally a one-pot meal.

Serves 6 | Prep. time 20 minutes | Cooking time 4 hours

Ingredients
2 pounds skin-on chicken thighs
1 tablespoon olive oil
1 cup mushrooms, quartered
3 carrots, chopped
1 small jar Kalamata olives
2 (14-ounce) cans diced tomatoes
1 small can tomato paste
1 cup red wine
5 garlic cloves, peeled and crushed
1 cup orzo

Directions
1. In a large skillet, heat the olive oil over medium-high heat. When the oil is heated, add the chicken, skin side down, and sear it. Make sure the pieces of chicken don't touch each other.
2. When the chicken is browned, add to the slow cooker along with all the ingredients except the orzo.
3. Cook the chicken on low for 2 hours, then add the orzo and cook for an additional 2 hours.
4. Serve with a crusty French bread.

Nutrition (per serving)
Calories 424, fat 16 g, carbs 64 g,
protein 11 g, sodium 551 mg

Beef and Veal Recipes

Tuscan Beef Stew

This delicious stew is imbued with the rich flavor of red wine and seasoning. Perfect for a cold winter day.

Serves 8 | Prep. time 10 minutes | Cooking time 4 hours

Ingredients
2 pounds beef stew meat, cut into 1½-inch cubes
4 carrots, cut into 1-inch chunks
2 (14½-ounce) cans diced tomatoes, undrained
1 medium onion, cut into wedges
1 package McCormick Slow Cookers Hearty Beef Stew Seasoning
½ cup water
½ cup dry red wine
1 teaspoon rosemary leaves, crushed
8 slices Italian bread, toasted

Directions
1. Place the cubed beef in the slow cooker along with the carrots, diced tomatoes, and onion wedges.
2. Mix the seasoning package in the ½ cup of water and stir well, making sure there are no lumps remaining.
3. Add the red wine to the water and stir slightly. Add the rosemary leaves to the water-and-wine mixture and then pour over the meat, stirring to ensure the meat is completely covered.
4. Turn the slow cooker to low and cook for 8 hours, or cook for 4 hours on high.
5. Serve with toasted Italian bread.

Nutrition (per serving)
Calories 329, fat 15 g, carbs 23 g, protein 25.6 g, sodium 947 mg

Cabbage Roll Casserole with Veal

This casserole deconstructs time-consuming cabbage rolls and allows you to cook them in the slow cooker for an easy, delicious supper. Using ground veal instead of beef adds an enticing layer of flavor that will make it hard to go back.

Serves 6 | Prep. time 5 minutes | Cooking time 4–8 hours

Ingredients
1 pound raw ground veal
1 head of cabbage, chopped
1 medium green pepper, chopped
1 medium onion, chopped
1 (15-ounce) can diced or stewed tomatoes, undrained
2 (15-ounce) cans tomato sauce
1 teaspoon minced garlic
1 tablespoon Worcestershire sauce
1 tablespoon beef bouillon
½ teaspoon salt
½ teaspoon pepper
1 cup uncooked brown rice

Directions
1. Add all the ingredients to your slow cooker
2. Stir well to combine.
3. Set your slow cooker to high and cook for 4 hours, or cook for 8 hours on low.

Nutrition (per serving)
Calories 335, fat 18.1 g, carbs 27.1 g, protein 22.9 g, sodium 499 mg

Mediterranean Beef Stew

This beef stew is low in carbohydrates and full of amazing layers of flavor for your taste buds. The rosemary, balsamic vinegar and garlic combine to capture the flavors of the Mediterranean in a one-dish meal that is sure to be a hit.

Serves 6 | Prep. time 25 minutes | Cooking time 8 hours

Ingredients
1 tablespoon olive oil
8 ounces sliced mushrooms
1 onion, diced into ½-inch pieces
2 pounds chuck roast, trimmed and cut into bite-sized cubes
1 cup beef stock
1 (14½-ounce) can diced tomatoes with juice
½ cup tomato sauce
¼ cup balsamic vinegar
1 can black olives, halved or quartered
½ cup garlic cloves, sliced thin
2 tablespoons fresh rosemary, finely chopped
2 tablespoons fresh parsley, finely chopped
1 tablespoon capers
fresh ground black pepper and salt to taste

Directions
1. Heat a skillet over high heat. Add 1 tablespoon of olive oil. Once the olive oil is heated, add the cubed roast and brown over high heat.
2. After the meat has browned, add the rest of the olive oil (if needed), then toss in the onions and mushrooms. When they have softened, transfer to the slow cooker.
3. Add the beef stock to the skillet to deglaze the pan, then pour it over the meat in the slow cooker. The bits left in the skillet will add some extra flavor to your stew.

4. Add the rest of the ingredients to the slow cooker and stir well to coat.
5. Set the temperature on your slow cooker to low and cook for 8 hours. You can cook on high for 4 hours if you're pressed for time, but this stew benefits from the long and slow method.

Nutrition (per serving)
Calories 471, fat 23.4 g, carbs 13.9 g,
protein 47.1 g, sodium 504 mg

Slow Cooked Daube Provencal

This traditional French stew is full of bold flavors. Everyone will love the pure comfort they feel when sitting down to this enticing meal.

Serves 8–10 | Prep. time 15 minutes | 4–8 hours

Ingredients
1 tablespoon olive oil
10 garlic cloves, minced
2 pounds boneless chuck roast, trimmed and cut into 2-inch cubes
1½ teaspoons salt, divided
½ teaspoon freshly ground black pepper
1 cup dry red wine
2 cups carrots, chopped
1½ cups onion, chopped
½ cup beef broth
1 (14-ounce) can diced tomatoes
1 tablespoon tomato paste
1 teaspoon fresh rosemary, chopped
1 teaspoon fresh thyme, chopped
½ teaspoon orange zest, grated
½ teaspoon ground cinnamon
¼ teaspoon ground cloves
1 bay leaf

Directions
1. Heat a skillet and then add the olive oil. Add the minced garlic and onions and cook until the onions are soft and the garlic begins to brown.
2. Add the cubed meat, salt, and pepper and cook until the meat has browned.
3. Transfer the meat to the slow cooker.

4. Add the beef broth to the skillet and let simmer for about 3 minutes to deglaze the pan, then pour into slow cooker over the meat.
5. Add the rest of the ingredients to the slow cooker and stir well to combine.
6. Set your slow cooker to low and cook for 8 hours, or set to high and cook for 4 hours.
7. Serve with a side of egg noodles, rice or some crusty Italian bread.

Nutrition (per serving)
Calories 547, fat 30.5 g, carbs 13 g,
protein 45.2 g, sodium 784 mg

Osso Bucco

This recipe enables you to make Osso Bucco in your slow cooker without losing any of the rich, deep flavor associated with this dish. The meat becomes fall-off-the-bone tender, and serving it with quinoa instead of rice adds health benefits associated with the Mediterranean diet.

Serves 2–4 | Prep. time 30 minutes | Cooking time 8 hours

Ingredients
4 beef shanks or veal shanks
1 teaspoon sea salt
½ teaspoon ground black pepper
3 tablespoons whole wheat flour
1–2 tablespoons olive oil
2 medium onions, diced
2 medium carrots, diced
2 celery stalks, diced
4 garlic cloves, minced
1 (14-ounce) can diced tomatoes
2 teaspoons dried thyme leaves
½ cup beef or vegetable stock

Directions
1. Season the shanks with salt and pepper on both sides, then dip in the flour to coat.
2. Heat a large skillet over high heat. Add the olive oil. When the oil is hot, add the shanks and brown evenly on both sides. When browned, transfer to the slow cooker.
3. Pour the stock into the skillet and let simmer for 3–5 minutes while stirring to deglaze the pan.
4. Add the rest of the ingredients to the slow cooker and pour the stock from the skillet over the top.

5. Set the slow cooker to low and cook for 8 hours.
6. Serve the Osso Bucco over quinoa, brown rice, or even cauliflower rice.

Nutrition (per serving)
Calories 589, fat 21.3 g, carbs 14.8 g,
protein 74.7 g, sodium 341 mg

Slow Cooker Beef Bourguignon

The wine in this dish adds a full and robust flavor that will have everyone begging for the recipe.

Serves 6–8 | Prep. time 5 minutes | Cooking time 6–8 hours

Ingredients
1 tablespoon extra-virgin olive oil
6 ounces bacon, roughly chopped
3 pounds beef brisket, trimmed of fat (chuck steak or stewing beef), cut into 2-inch cubes
1 large carrot, sliced
1 large white onion, diced
6 cloves garlic, minced and divided
½ teaspoon coarse salt
½ teaspoon freshly ground pepper
2 tablespoons whole wheat
12 small pearl onions
3 cups red wine (Merlot, Pinot Noir, or Chianti)
2 cups beef stock
2 tablespoons tomato paste
1 beef bouillon cube, crushed
1 teaspoon fresh thyme, finely chopped
2 tablespoons fresh parsley, finely chopped and divided
2 bay leaves
2 tablespoons butter or 1 tablespoon olive oil
1 pound fresh small white or brown mushrooms, quartered

Directions
1. Heat a skillet over medium-high heat, then add the olive oil. When the oil has heated, cook the bacon until it is crisp, then place it in your slow cooker. Save the bacon fat in the skillet.
2. Dry the beef with a paper towel and cook it in the same skillet with the bacon fat until all sides have the same brown coloring.
3. Transfer to the slow cooker.
4. Add the onions and carrots to the slow cooker and season with the salt and pepper. Stir to combine the ingredients and make sure everything is seasoned.
5. Pour the red wine into the skillet and simmer for 4–5 minutes to deglaze the pan, then whisk in the flour, stirring until smooth. Continue cooking until the liquid reduces and thickens a bit.
6. When the liquid has thickened, pour it into the slow cooker and stir to coat everything with the wine mixture. Add the tomato paste, bouillon cube, thyme, parsley, 4 cloves of garlic, and bay leaf.
7. Set your slow cooker to high and cook for 6 hours, or set to low and cook for 8 hours.
8. Just before you are ready to serve, melt the butter or heat the olive oil in a skillet over medium heat. When the oil is hot, add the remaining 2 cloves of garlic and cook for about 1 minute before adding the mushrooms.
9. Cook the mushrooms until soft, then add to the slow cooker and mix to combine.
10. Serve with mashed potatoes, rice or noodles.

Nutrition (per serving)
Calories 672, fat 32 g, carbs 17 g,
protein 56 g, sodium 620 mg

Balsamic Beef

Serves 8–10 | Prep. time 5 minutes | Cooking time 8 hours

Ingredients
2 pounds boneless chuck roast
1 tablespoon olive oil

Rub
1 teaspoon garlic powder
½ teaspoon onion powder
1 teaspoon sea salt
½ teaspoon freshly ground black pepper

Sauce
½ cup balsamic vinegar
2 tablespoons honey
1 tablespoon honey mustard
1 cup beef broth
1 tablespoon tapioca, whole wheat flour, or cornstarch (to thicken sauce when it is done cooking if desired)

Directions
1. Mix together all of the ingredients for the rub.
2. In a separate bowl, mix the balsamic vinegar, honey, honey mustard, and beef broth.
3. Coat the roast in olive oil, then rub in the spices from the rub mix.
4. Place the roast in the slow cooker and then pour the sauce over the top.
5. Set the slow cooker to low and cook for 8 hours.

6. If you want to thicken the sauce when the roast is done cooking transfer it from the slow cooker to a serving plate. Then pour the liquid into a saucepan and heat to boiling on the stovetop. Whisk in the flour until smooth and let simmer until the sauce thickens.

Nutrition (per serving)
Calories 306, fat 19 g, carbs 5.7 g,
protein 25 g, sodium 364 mg

Veal Pot Roast

This elegant veal roast recipe is perfect for Sunday dinner. The seasoned veal should be juicy and full of flavor after its five hours in the slow cooker. Filled with vitamins and minerals, the root vegetables offer a healthy addition.

Serves 6–8 | Prep. time 20 minutes | Cooking time 5 hours

Ingredients
2 tablespoons olive oil
Salt and pepper
3-pound boneless veal roast, tied
4 medium carrots, peeled
2 parsnips, peeled and halved
2 white turnips, peeled and quartered
10 garlic cloves, peeled
2 sprigs fresh thyme
1 orange, scrubbed and zested
1 cup chicken or veal stock

Directions
1. Heat a large skillet over medium-high heat.
2. Rub veal roast all over with olive oil, then season with salt and pepper.
3. When the skillet is hot, add the veal roast and sear on all sides. This will take about 3 minutes on every side, but this process seals in the juices and makes the meat succulent.
4. When the roast is brown on all sides, transfer it to the slow cooker.
5. Toss the carrots, parsnips, turnips, and garlic into the skillet. Stir and cook for about 5 minutes—not all the way through, just to get some of the brown bits from the veal and give them a bit of color.

6. Transfer the vegetables to the slow cooker, placing them all around the meat.
7. Top the roast with the thyme and the zest from the orange. Cut the orange in half and squeeze the juice over the top of the meat.
8. Add the chicken stock, then cook the roast on low for 5 hours.

Nutrition (per serving)
Calories 426, fat 12.8 g, carbs 30.7g,
protein 48.8 g, sodium 778 mg

Pork and Lamb Recipes

Mediterranean Rice and Sausage

This sausage and rice recipe is very quick and easy, making it perfect to throw together before you leave for work. When you get home, simply add the rice and a hearty supper is ready in 20 minutes.

Serves 6 | Prep. time 15 minutes| Cook time 8 hours

Ingredients
1½ pounds Italian sausage, crumbled
1 medium onion, chopped
2 tablespoons steak sauce
2 cups long grain rice, uncooked
1 (14-ounce) can diced tomatoes with juice
½ cup water
1 medium green pepper, diced

Directions
1. Spray your slow cooker with olive oil or nonstick cooking spray.
2. Add the sausage, onion, and steak sauce to the slow cooker.
3. Cook on low for 8 to 10 hours.
4. After 8 hours, add the rice, tomatoes, water and green pepper. Stir to combine thoroughly.
5. Cook an additional 20 to 25 minutes or until the rice is cooked.

Nutrition (per serving)
Calories 650, fat 36 g, carbs 57 g,
protein 22 g, sodium 1010 mg

Lamb Shanks with Red Wine

These lamb shanks are easy to prepare in the slow cooker and make for a deliciously fall-off-the-bone tender Sunday dinner. Enjoy over pasta or whole grain wild rice.

Serves 4 | Prep. time 20 minutes | Cook time 5 hours

Ingredients
2 tablespoons olive oil
2 tablespoons flour
4 lamb shanks, trimmed
1 onion, chopped
2 garlic cloves, crushed
⅔ cup red wine
3 cups tomato sauce

Directions
1. Heat a skillet over high heat. Add the olive oil.
2. Season the lamb shanks with salt and pepper and then roll in the flour. Shake off excess flour and place the shanks in the skillet to brown on all sides.
3. Spray the slow cooker with olive oil and place the browned shanks in the slow cooker.
4. Add the crushed garlic to the red wine. Mix with the tomato sauce and then pour the mixture over the lamb shanks and cook on low for 5–6 hours or until shanks are fall-off-the-bone tender.

Nutrition (per serving)
Calories 354, fat 12 g, carbs 18.1 g,
protein 41.8 g, sodium 487 mg

Spanish Meatballs

These amazing meatballs are delicious served on their own, with a nice crusty bread as a sandwich, or with your favorite marinara sauce over pasta.

Serves 6 | Prep. time 20 minutes | Cook time 5 hours

Ingredients
1 pound ground turkey
1 pound ground pork
2 eggs
1 (20-ounce) can diced tomatoes
¾ cup sweet onion, minced, divided
¼ cup plus 1 tablespoon breadcrumbs
3 tablespoons fresh parsley, chopped
1½ teaspoons cumin
1½ teaspoons paprika (sweet or hot)

Directions
1. Spray the slow cooker with olive oil.
2. In a mixing bowl, combine the ground meat, eggs, about half of the onions, the breadcrumbs, and the spices.
3. Wash your hands and mix together until everything is well combined. Do not over-mix, though, as this makes for tough meatballs. Shape into meatballs. How big you make them will obviously determine how many total meatballs you get.
4. In a skillet, heat 2 tablespoons of olive oil over medium heat. When the skillet and oil are hot, add the meatballs and brown on all sides. Make sure the balls aren't touching each other so they brown evenly. When they are done, transfer them to the slow cooker.

5. Add the rest of the onions and the tomatoes to the skillet and allow them to cook for a few minutes, scraping the brown bits from the meatballs up to add flavor.
6. Pour the tomatoes over the meatballs in the slow cooker and cook on low for 5 hours.

Nutrition (per serving)
Calories 372, fat 21.7 g, carbs 15.1 g, protein 28.5 g, sodium 475 mg

Leg of Lamb with Rosemary and Garlic

This rich, flavorful leg of lamb recipe is easy enough to make every day, yet elegant enough to serve at a dinner party. Whenever you choose to prepare it, it will definitely be a crowd pleaser.

Serves 4–6 | Prep. time 15 minutes | Cooking time 8 hours

Ingredients
3–4-pound leg of lamb
4 garlic cloves, sliced thin
5–8 sprigs fresh rosemary (more if desired)
2 tablespoons olive oil
1 lemon, halved
¼ cup flour

Directions
1. Heat a skillet over high heat and add the olive oil.
2. When the olive oil is hot, add the leg of lamb and sear on both sides until brown.
3. Spray the slow cooker with olive oil and then transfer the lamb to the slow cooker.
4. Squeeze the lemon over the meat and then place in the pot next to the lamb.
5. Take a sharp knife and make small incisions in the meat, then stuff the holes you created with rosemary and garlic.
6. Place any remaining rosemary and garlic on top of the roast.
7. Cook on low for 8 hours.

Nutrition (per serving)
Calories 557, fat 39 g, carbs 1.4 g,
protein 46.4 g, sodium 143 mg

Lemon Honey Lamb Shoulder

Another simple yet elegant recipe that will have everyone singing your accolades. A perfect meal for any time you need to impress.

Serves 4 | Prep. time 10 minutes | Cooking time 8 hours

Ingredients
3 cloves garlic, thinly sliced
1 tablespoon fresh rosemary, chopped
1 teaspoon lemon zest, grated
½ teaspoon each salt and pepper
4–5-pound boneless lamb shoulder roast
3 tablespoons lemon juice
1 tablespoon honey
6 shallots, quartered
2 teaspoons cornstarch

Directions
1. In a small bowl, mix together the garlic, rosemary, lemon zest, salt, and pepper. Stir to combine.
2. Rub the spice mixture into the lamb shoulder. Make sure to coat the whole roast.
3. Spray the slow cooker with olive oil and add the lamb.
4. Mix together the honey and lemon juice and then pour over the meat.
5. Arrange the shallots beside the meat in the slow cooker. You can also add any root vegetables you would like.
6. Cook on low for 8 hours.
7. Serve. You can make a gravy by transferring the juice from the slow cooker to a medium saucepan. Thoroughly mix the cornstarch into a little water until smooth. Then mix into the juice and bring to a simmer. Simmer until mixture thickens.

Nutrition (per serving)
Calories 240, fat 11 g, carbs 5 g,
protein 31 g, sodium 241 mg

Italian Shredded Pork Stew

This Italian stew is a bit different from your average stew, full of hearty vegetables and aromatic spices. Your mouth will be watering long before it's done cooking. Easy to put together, this stew is perfect any day of the week.

Serves 8 | Prep. time 20 minutes | Cooking time 8 hours

Ingredients
2 medium sweet potatoes, peeled and cubed
2 cups fresh kale, chopped
1 large onion, chopped
4 cloves garlic, minced
1 2½–3½ pound boneless pork shoulder butt roast
1 (14-ounce) can cannellini beans, rinsed and drained
1½ teaspoons Italian seasoning
½ teaspoon salt
½ teaspoon pepper
3 (14½-ounce) cans chicken broth
Sour cream (optional)

Directions
1. Spray your slow cooker with nonstick cooking spray or olive oil.
2. Place the cubed sweet potatoes, kale, garlic and onion into the slow cooker.
3. Add the pork shoulder on top of the potatoes.
4. Add the beans, Italian seasoning salt, and pepper.
5. Pour the chicken broth over the meat.
6. Cook on low for 8 hours.
7. Serve with sour cream, if desired.

Nutrition (per serving)
Calories 283, fat 13 g, carbs 15 g,
protein 24 g, sodium 860 mg

Parmesan Honey Pork Loin Roast

Serves 6–8 | Prep. time 10 minutes | Cooking time 5 hours

Ingredients
3-pound pork loin
⅔ cup grated parmesan cheese
½ cup honey
3 tablespoons soy sauce
1 tablespoon oregano
1 tablespoon basil
2 tablespoons garlic, chopped
2 tablespoons olive oil
½ teaspoon salt
2 tablespoons cornstarch
¼ cup chicken broth

Directions
1. Spray your slow cooker with olive oil or nonstick cooking spray.
2. Place the pork loin in the slow cooker.
3. In a small mixing bowl, combine the cheese, honey, soy sauce, oregano, basil, garlic, olive oil, and salt. Stir with a fork to combine well, then pour over the pork loin.
4. Cook on low for 5–6 hours or until roast is done.
5. Remove the pork loin and put on a serving platter.
6. Pour the juices from the slow cooker into a small saucepan. You can strain out the bits if you like, but it is good like it is.
7. Create a slurry by mixing the cornstarch into the chicken broth and whisking until smooth.
8. Bring the contents of the saucepan to a boil, then whisk in the slurry and let simmer until thickened. Pour over the pork loin and serve.

Nutrition (per serving)
Calories 449, fat 15 g, carbs 21 g,
protein 55 g, sodium 789 mg

Braised Pork Loin with Port and Dried Plums

This is a fantastic recipe! The flavors from this dish are so tasty that everyone will want a second helping.

Serves 10 | Prep. time 15 minutes | Cooking time 6 hours

Ingredients
1 3¼-pound boneless pork loin roast, trimmed
1½ teaspoons freshly ground black pepper
1 teaspoon salt
1 teaspoon dry mustard
1 teaspoon dried sage (not rubbed sage)
½ teaspoon dried thyme
1 tablespoon olive oil
2 cups onion, sliced
1 cup leek, finely chopped
1 cup carrot, diced
½ cup port wine (or any sweet red wine)
⅓ cup chicken broth
1 cup pitted dried plums
2 bay leaves
2 tablespoons cornstarch
2 tablespoons water

Directions
1. Spray the slow cooker with olive oil.
2. Cut the pork loin in half down the middle (not lengthwise).
3. Combine the pepper, salt, dry mustard, sage, and thyme and rub over both halves of the roast.
4. Heat the olive oil in a large skillet. When hot, add each half of the pork roast and brown thoroughly on both sides.

5. Transfer the meat to the slow cooker. Add the onions, leeks, and carrots. Cook for about 5 minutes, stirring frequently. Make sure to scrape up the brown bits left from browning the meat.
6. Pour in the wine, broth and ⅓ cup of water. Let this simmer for a bit until the liquid reduces a little. Stir again to make sure the pan has been deglazed.
7. Pour the contents of the skillet over the pork loin in the slow cooker.
8. Add the dried plums and bay leaves. Cook on low for 6 hours.
9. When the meat is done, remove from the slow cooker and place on a serving platter. Combine the cornstarch and 2 tablespoons of water, then stir into the liquid in the slow cooker. Continue cooking until the liquid starts to thicken. (You can also thicken the liquid in a separate saucepan.)

Nutrition (per serving)
Calories 280, fat 7.8 g, carbs 17.7 g,
protein 32.2 g, sodium 340 mg

Fish and Seafood Recipes

Seafood Cioppino

Most people don't think of seafood recipes for the slow cooker. This cioppino is a perfect recipe to experience the brilliance of using a slow cooker to prepare seafood. It will bring your taste buds on a tour of San Francisco, where the dish is a popular choice.

Serves 6–8 | Prep. time 10 minutes | Cooking time 5 hours

Ingredients
1 (15-ounce) can diced tomatoes, undrained
1 red bell pepper, chopped
2 medium onions, chopped
3 celery stalks, chopped
2 cups seafood/fish stock
6 ounces tomato paste
½ cup white wine (or additional seafood stock)
1 tablespoon garlic, minced
2 teaspoons Italian seasoning
1 teaspoon sugar
1 bay leaf
¾ teaspoon crushed red pepper flakes (optional)
12 ounces solid white albacore in water, drained
1 pound cooked shrimp, peeled and deveined
12 ounces lump crabmeat, drained
6 ounces chopped clams, drained
2 tablespoons fresh basil, chopped
1 tablespoon fresh parsley, chopped
Salt and pepper, to taste

Directions
1. Spray your slow cooker with olive oil.
2. Place the following ingredients into the slow cooker: tomatoes, pepper, onions, celery, seafood stock, tomato paste, white wine, garlic, Italian seasoning, sugar, bay leaf, and red pepper flakes.
3. Cook on low for 4–6 hours.
4. Add the tuna, shrimp, crabmeat, and clams. Stir until well combined, then cook for about another 10 minutes. You are just heating the seafood through.
5. When the seafood has heated, add the basil and parsley.

Nutrition (per serving)
Calories 237, fat 5 g, carbs 10 g,
protein 33 g, sodium 1364 mg

Shrimp Scampi

It may seem like overkill to make shrimp scampi in a slow cooker, but when you can put everything together in one pot and forget about it for an hour and a half, it's worth it. Delicious over pasta or with a loaf of your favorite crusty bread.

Serves 4 | Prep. time 10 minutes | Cooking time 1 h 30 min

Ingredients
⅓ cup chicken broth
2 tablespoons olive oil
2 tablespoons butter
1 tablespoon minced garlic
2 tablespoons parsley or 2 teaspoons dried
½ freshly squeezed lemon
Salt and pepper, to taste
1 ½ pounds raw shrimp, peeled & deveined (but leave the tail on while cooking)

Directions
1. Add everything but the shrimp to the slow cooker and stir to combine.
2. Mix in the raw shrimp.
3. Cook on high for 1½ hours.
4. Serve with pasta or a nice crunchy Italian bread.

Nutrition (per serving)
Calories 340, fat 19.5 g, carbs 2 g,
protein 36.8 g, sodium 384 mg

Tilapia Pesto

The great thing about seafood in the slow cooker is that it isn't an all-day cook time. These foil-wrapped tilapia fillets can be made up ahead of time and stored in the freezer until ready to use or cooked immediately in half the time.

Serves 4 | Prep. time 10 minutes | Cooking time 2–4 hours

Ingredients
1 cup pesto
4 tilapia fillets
¼ cup tomato paste
1 cup onion, diced
1 teaspoon salt
½ teaspoon black pepper
1 medium lemon, sliced

Directions
1. You are going to cook these fillets in four separate foil packets, so lay a sheet (or four) of aluminum foil on the countertop.
2. Spread ¼ cup of pesto in the center of each sheet of foil.
3. Place 1 fillet on top of each layer of pesto.
4. Spread 1 tablespoon of tomato paste across each fillet.
5. Place ¼ cup onion over the tomato paste.
6. Salt and pepper each fillet to taste.
7. Place a couple of slices of lemon over each fillet.
8. Seal the foil packets by folding tightly. Now you can place the packets into freezer bags and freeze or cook immediately.
9. If cooking now, cook on low for 2 hours.
10. If cooking from frozen, cook on low for 4 hours.

Nutrition (per serving)
Calories 420, fat 28 g, carbs 9 g,
protein 32 g, sodium 1270 mg

Seafood Stew

This seafood stew recipe will bring a taste of the ocean to wherever you live. Light enough for a hot summer day but filling enough for any time of the year.

Serves 4–6 | Prep. time 10 minutes | Cooking time 5 hours

Ingredients
1¾ pounds crushed tomatoes
4 cups vegetable broth
½ cup white wine
3 cloves garlic, minced
1 pound Dutch baby potatoes or other white/yellow baby potatoes, cut into bite-sized pieces
½ medium onion, diced (about ½ cup)
1 teaspoon dried thyme
1 teaspoon dried basil
1 teaspoon dried cilantro
½ teaspoon celery salt
½ teaspoon salt
½ teaspoon pepper
¼ teaspoon red pepper flakes
Pinch cayenne pepper
2 pounds seafood (I used scallops, extra-large shrimp and crab legs)

Directions
1. Add everything except the seafood to your slow cooker.
2. Cook on high for 2 hours or low for 4 hours.
3. Add the seafood to the slow cooker and cook for an additional 30 to 60 minutes or until the seafood is fully cooked.

Nutrition (per serving)
Calories 236, fat 1 g, carbs 31 g,
protein 22 g, sodium 1789 mg

Lemon Dill Salmon

The health benefits of salmon are one of the perks that make this dish so appealing, but it's the lemon and dill that create a bright flavor combination to satisfy your hunger.

Serves 4–6 | Prep. time 20 minutes | Cooking time 50 minutes

Ingredients
1-pound salmon fillet, cut into 4 portions
Salt and pepper
Juice from 2 lemons
2 sprigs fresh dill, finely chopped

Directions
1. Line your slow cooker with a large sheet of parchment paper.
2. Lay the salmon flat on top of the parchment paper. Try not to overlap the pieces. You may have to cut the fillets into smaller pieces to get them to fit.
3. Sprinkle the fillets with salt and pepper and dill, then squeeze on the lemon juice.
4. Cook on high for about an hour or until the salmon is flaky. Carefully lift the parchment paper out of the slow cooker and transfer the salmon to a serving dish.

Nutrition (per serving)
Calories 168, fat 7.1 g, carbs 3.2 g, protein 22.3 g, sodium 721 mg

Seafood Paella

This classic dish from Spain is loaded with spice. It is an amazing and delightful idea for dinner any day of the week.

Serves 6 | Prep. time 10 minutes | Cooking time 2 hours

Ingredients
1 teaspoon extra-virgin olive oil
1½ pounds boneless skinless chicken breasts, cubed
½ pound sliced chorizo
Kosher salt and freshly ground black pepper, to taste
1 cup uncooked long-grain rice
1 (15-ounce) can diced tomatoes, undrained
1 large yellow onion, peeled and chopped
4 cloves garlic, peeled and minced
2 teaspoons paprika
¼ teaspoon cayenne pepper
2 cups reduced-sodium chicken broth
⅓ cup dry white wine
½ pound raw medium shrimp, peeled and deveined
1½ cups frozen peas, thawed and drained
Fresh parsley, chopped, for garnish
Lemon wedges, for serving

Directions
1. In a large skillet, heat olive oil over medium-high heat. When the skillet is hot, add the chicken and chorizo. Cook until chicken is brown and chorizo is cooked.
2. Transfer the chicken and chorizo to the slow cooker and sprinkle with salt and pepper.
3. Add the uncooked rice, tomatoes, onion, garlic, and all of the spices, followed by the chicken broth and wine. Stir a couple of times to mix well.

4. Cook on high for an hour and a half, then add the shrimp and the peas. Stir those in, then cook for 30 more minutes.
5. Serve when the shrimp is cooked through.

Nutrition (per serving)
Calories 274, fat 11 g, carbs 22 g,
protein 21.7 g, sodium 1118 mg

Vegetarian Recipes

Turkish Stuffed Eggplant

This recipe is a delicious way to utilize your slow cooker in a completely vegetarian dish. The stuffed eggplant makes for an impressive meal to serve guests.

Serves 4 | Prep. time 15 minutes | Cooking time 5 hours

Ingredients
2 (10-ounce) Italian eggplants
1 onion, diced
3–4 cloves garlic, minced or pressed
½ cup cooked bulgur or quinoa
1 (14.5-ounce) can fire roasted or Italian seasoned diced tomatoes
2 cups fresh spinach
½ teaspoon dried oregano
¼ teaspoon cumin
⅛ teaspoon cayenne pepper (optional)
1 tablespoon sherry or red-wine vinegar
¼ cup Parmesan cheese, grated
¼ teaspoon kosher salt
Black pepper, to taste

Directions
1. Place the onions, garlic, tomatoes, oregano, cumin, cayenne pepper and red wine vinegar in the slow cooker.
2. Cut the eggplants in half lengthwise and place them into the slow cooker with the cut side down.
3. Cook on low for 5–6 hours.

4. When eggplant is done, remove from the slow cooker and use the back of a spoon to press the soft flesh down to make a pocket.
5. In a mixing bowl, combine the cooked bulgur or quinoa, the fresh spinach, and the parmesan cheese. Mix into the tomato mixture in the slow cooker. Stir well to combine and let sit for about 3–5 minutes or until the spinach is soft.
6. Spoon the mixture into the eggplants and serve.

Nutrition (per serving)
Calories 291, fat 20.7 g, carbs 13.8 g,
protein 14.2 g, sodium 667 mg

Greek Rice

This colorful rice makes a delicious vegetarian meal which can also be served as a hearty side dish. Adding a can of chickpeas to the ingredient list provides a protein boost.

Serves 6 | Prep. time 10 minutes | Cooking time 2 hours

Ingredients
1 tablespoon plus 1 teaspoon olive oil
2 cups uncooked rice
1 onion, chopped fine
1 tablespoon garlic, minced
1 teaspoon Greek seasoning
1 teaspoon dried oregano
2 (14-ounce) cans chicken or vegetable stock plus enough water to make 4 cups
1 red bell pepper, seeded and finely chopped
1 green bell pepper, seeded and finely chopped
¾ cup sliced Kalamata olives
1 cup crumbled Feta cheese + ½ cup more for sprinkling on top if desired
¼ cup sliced green onion (or more)
1–2 tablespoons fresh-squeezed lemon juice
Salt and fresh-ground black pepper, to taste

Directions
1. In a large skillet, heat 1 tablespoon of olive oil over high heat. When hot, add the rice and cook, stirring constantly until it starts to brown. When brown, add to the slow cooker.
2. Add the rest of the oil to the skillet and cook the onion, garlic, Greek seasoning and oregano until the onion is clear.

3. Add 1 cup of the stock to the skillet to deglaze, then pour into the slow cooker along with the rest of the liquid and the pepper and olives.
4. Cook on high for about an hour and a half.
5. When the rice is tender, stir in the cup of feta cheese and the green onion.
6. Serve with the remaining feta. Squeeze lemon over the top and add salt and pepper to taste.

Nutrition (per serving)
Calories 269, fat 17.1 g, carbs 25.2 g,
protein 6 g, sodium 297 mg

Slow Cooker Ratatouille

This recipe for slow-cooked vegetables is so tasty you will never miss the meat. It can be eaten as a meal or as a side to complement any meat dish.

Serves 8 | Prep. time 10 minutes | Cooking time 6 hours

Ingredients
3 tablespoons olive oil
2 medium yellow onions, diced
1 pound eggplant, trimmed and cut into 1-inch cubes
1 pound zucchini or summer squash, cut into 1 inch cubes
2 large red, green, or yellow bell peppers, cleaned and chopped into pieces
1 pound tomatoes, washed and cut into cubes
4 cloves garlic, diced
2 tablespoons tomato paste
½ teaspoon fine salt, plus more for seasoning
¼ cup fresh basil leaves, coarsely chopped (plus more for garnish)

Directions
1. Place all ingredients into the slow cooker and cook on low for 6 hours.
2. When vegetables are very soft, serve with fresh basil.

Nutrition (per serving)
Calories 159, fat 7.7 g, carbs 22.3 g,
protein 4.4 g, sodium 434 mg

Chickpea Curry

This high protein dish is a perfect meatless meal. The slow cooker does all the work, so you are free to go about your day.

Serves 4–6 | Prep. time 5 minutes | Cooking time 6–8 hours

Ingredients
2 onions, diced
4 cloves garlic, minced
1 inch ginger, minced
2 (15-ounce) cans chickpeas
1 (15-ounce) can diced tomatoes
1 (15-ounce) can coconut milk
1–2 tablespoons curry powder
Salt, to taste
½ bunch cilantro
Basmati rice, for serving

Directions
1. Mix everything except for the cilantro together in the slow cooker.
2. Cook on low for 6–8 hours.
3. Just before serving, mix in the cilantro. Serve over rice.

Nutrition (per serving)
Calories 216, fat 7.5 g, carbs 32.5 g,
protein 7.4 g, sodium 510 mg

Eggplant Parmigiana

This take on the original eggplant parmigiana is perfect to serve to company. They will think you spent all day in the kitchen when in truth, the slow cooker did all the work.

Serves 8 | Prep. time 24 minutes | Cooking time 8 hours

Ingredients
4 pounds eggplant
1 tablespoon salt
3 large eggs
¼ cup milk of choice
1½ cup breadcrumbs
3 ounces Parmesan cheese
2 teaspoons Italian seasoning
4 cups marinara sauce, divided
1 pound mozzarella cheese, sliced or shredded
Fresh basil, for topping

Directions
1. Whisk together the eggs and milk. In a separate bowl, mix the breadcrumbs and parmesan cheese.
2. Peel and cut the eggplant into equal size rounds.
3. Season the eggplant with salt and pepper.
4. Dip the eggplant rounds into the egg-and-milk mixture, then into the breadcrumbs mixed with the parmesan cheese.
5. Pour 2 cups of the marinara sauce into the slow cooker.
6. Place the breaded eggplant slices in the slow cooker. Add a layer of mozzarella and another cup of the marinara sauce. Repeat the layers using the remaining eggplant rounds.

7. Sprinkle the top with the remaining mozzarella and cook on low for 8 hours.
8. Serve with the fresh basil.

Nutrition (per serving)
Calories 258, fat 12 g, carbs 23 g, protein 16 g, sodium 1380 mg

Slow Cooked Caponata

Caponata is a sweet and sour dish that originated in Sicily. This a very satisfying meal to come home to after a long day at work.

Serves 4–6 | Prep. time 5 minutes | Cooking time 2½ hours

Ingredients
¼ cup extra virgin olive oil
2 cloves garlic, minced
1 medium eggplant (about 1 pound), cut into small cubes
1 medium sweet onion, diced
6 Roma tomatoes, seeded and chopped
2 celery ribs, diced
¼ cup tomato paste
¼ cup water
1 teaspoon kosher salt
¼ teaspoon red chili flakes
½ cup golden raisins
¼ cup capers, drained and rinsed
1 tablespoon granulated sugar
2 tablespoons toasted pine nuts
½ cup red wine vinegar
2 tablespoons flat leaf parsley, minced
Kosher salt and freshly cracked black pepper, to taste

Directions
1. Put the olive oil, garlic, eggplant, onion, tomatoes, celery, tomato paste, water, 1 teaspoon salt, and red chili flakes into the slow cooker. Stir together until well combined. Cook on high for 1 hour.
2. Stir in the raisins, capers, sugar, pine nuts, and vinegar, then cook for an additional 1½ hours.
3. Serve with a sprinkling of parsley.

Nutrition (per serving)
Calories 177, fat 12.5 g, carbs 13.4 g,
protein 2.6 g, sodium 189 mg

Soup Recipes

Minestrone Soup

Soups are a perfect choice for your slow cooker. This traditional minestrone soup is a delicious start to your meal that can also stand alone as an entree.

Serves 4–6 | Prep. time 10 minutes | Cooking time 6 hours 25 minutes

Ingredients
2 (14½-ounce) cans diced tomatoes
2 tablespoons tomato paste
¼ cup sun-dried tomato pesto
1 parmesan rind
4 cups vegetable stock
2 cups water
1 cup carrots, diced
1¼ cups celery, diced
1½ cups white onion, diced
4–5 cloves garlic, minced
1 teaspoon dried oregano
1 sprig rosemary (or ½ teaspoon dried)
2 bay leaves
Salt and pepper, to taste
1 (15-ounce) can red kidney beans, drained and rinsed
1 (15-ounce) can Great Northern beans, drained and rinsed
1½ cups zucchini, diced
1½ cups tubular pasta, cooked
1 cup frozen green beans, thawed
2½ cups baby spinach, chopped
Finely shredded Parmesan cheese, for serving

Directions
1. Add everything but the pasta and spinach to the slow cooker and cook on low for 6–8 hours.
2. Add the cooked pasta and the spinach and cook for an additional 25 minutes.
3. Serve with shredded parmesan.

Nutrition (per serving)
Calories 307, fat 9.8 g, carbs 44.2 g,
protein 12.8 g, sodium 470 mg

Tuscan Cannellini Bean Soup

This slow-cooked Tuscan soup is full of protein and health benefits, But the best part is that it's delicious and easy to prepare.

Serves 6–8 | Prep. time 30 minutes | Cooking time 8 hours

Ingredients
½ pound Italian sausage
2 onions, chopped
3 cloves garlic, minced
2 tablespoons tomato paste
3½ cups chicken broth
½ cup dry white wine (or more chicken broth)
1 (14½-ounce) can diced tomatoes
1 (15-ounce) can tomato sauce
2 carrots, peeled and sliced
3 stalks celery, sliced
1 green pepper, diced
2 tablespoons dried Italian herbs
2 sprigs fresh rosemary (optional)
½ cup roasted red peppers, diced
½ cup orzo, uncooked
½ teaspoon salt
1 (15-ounce) can white beans, rinsed and drained
2 cups baby spinach or chopped kale

Directions
1. In a large skillet, brown the sausage and then mix in the onions and garlic. When brown, transfer to the slow cooker.
2. Put the white wine, tomato paste, and 1 cup of chicken broth into the skillet and deglaze. Make sure to get the brown bits off.

3. Add the liquid from the skillet and all the remaining ingredients except for the spinach to the slow cooker and cook on low for 6–8 hours.
4. 20 minutes before serving, add the spinach to the slow cooker and stir well to combine.

Nutrition (per serving)
Calories 236, fat 6.1 g, carbs 25.7 g,
protein 16.9 g, sodium 728 mg

Moroccan Lentil Soup

This one-pot recipe is packed with the beautiful flavors of Morocco—as well as plenty of protein.

Serves 6 | Prep. time 15 minutes | Cooking time 6 hours

Ingredients
1½ cups green lentils
1 sweet onion, finely chopped
1-inch knob of fresh ginger, grated
2 cloves garlic, minced
3 carrots, chopped
1 red bell pepper, chopped
1 (14-ounce) can diced tomatoes
4 cups low sodium vegetable or chicken broth
1–2 tablespoons red harissa
2 teaspoons smoked paprika
¾ teaspoon cumin
¾ teaspoon cinnamon
Kosher salt and pepper, to taste
1 tablespoon fresh lemon juice
1 (14-ounce) can chickpeas
½ cup fresh cilantro
Goat cheese, chopped, whipped or crumbled, for serving (optional)

Directions
1. To your slow cooker, add all the ingredients except for the chickpeas and cilantro and cook on low for 6 hours.
2. 30 minutes before serving, add the chickpeas and cilantro and stir to combine.
3. Serve with goat cheese if desired.

Nutrition (per serving)
Calories 219, fat 1.2 g, carbs 40.8 g,
protein 11 g, sodium 982 mg

Italian Meatball Soup

This super-delicious meatball soup is full of vegetables and tastes amazing. It is low in calories and makes for a great meal on a cold day.

Serves 2 | Prep. time 15 minutes | Cooking time 6 hours

Ingredients
3 medium carrots, sliced
2 ribs celery, sliced
1 medium yellow onion, diced
1 teaspoon dried Italian seasoning
¼ teaspoon black pepper
1 bay leaf
12 ounces frozen Italian meatballs (the fully cooked kind)
4 cups beef broth
2 cups water
⅝ cup dry red wine
2 (15-ounce) cans diced tomatoes with Italian seasoning
¾ cup dry ditalini pasta (any small pasta will do)
3–5 ounces fresh baby spinach
Freshly grated Parmesan cheese, for serving

Directions
1. Place all ingredients except for the pasta and spinach in the slow cooker.
2. Cook on low for 6 hours.
3. Add the pasta and baby spinach and cook for an additional 30 minutes or until pasta is tender.
4. Serve with grated parmesan.

Nutrition (per serving)
Calories 170, fat 7 g, carbs 13 g,
protein 9 g, sodium 386 mg

Desserts

Cherry Clafoutis

This is a classic French dessert that tastes great and is easy to prepare in the slow cooker. Everyone will love the tartness of the cherries mixed with the creamy, custard-like cake.

Serves 6 | Prep. time 10 minutes | Cook time 3–4 hours

Ingredients
1 pound fresh cherries (or use a jar of cherries in natural juice or brandy, drained but with the juices retained)
¼ cup butter
4 large eggs
2 extra egg yolks
¾ cup white sugar
½ cup all-purpose flour, sifted
1⅓ cups whole milk

Directions
1. Remove the pot from your slow cooker and heat the base on high while you are preparing the ingredients.
2. Use 1 tablespoon of the butter to butter the sides of the pot, then melt the rest of the butter in the microwave and set aside to cool down.
3. In a mixing bowl, mix together the eggs, yolks, and sugar. Mix or whisk in the melted butter, flour, and the milk to form a light batter.
4. Pour the cherries into the buttered pot, then pour the batter over the top.
5. Cook on high for 3–4 hours or until the clafoutis is set.

Nutrition (per serving)
Calories 252, fat 9.8 g, carbs 34.2 g,
protein 6.8 g, sodium 142 mg

Brown Rice Pudding

Rice pudding is a delicious dessert that's a natural for slow cooker preparation. The use of brown rice in this recipe makes it a bit healthier, too.

Serves 4–6 | Prep. time 5 minutes | Cook time 3 hours

Ingredients
4 cups milk of your choice
¼ cup maple syrup
⅔ cup brown rice
1 cinnamon stick
1 teaspoon vanilla

Directions
1. Spray your slow cooker with nonstick cooking spray.
2. Add all the ingredients to the slow cooker and stir.
3. Cook on high for 3 hours.
4. Remove the cinnamon stick and serve.

Nutrition (per serving)
Calories 210, fat 1 g, carbs 42.4 g, protein 7.8 g, sodium 325 mg

Poached Pears in Red Wine

This elegant dessert recipe blends the sweetness of pears with the dry tartness of red wine to combine for a tasty and classy after-dinner meal.

Serves 6 | Prep. time 5 minutes | Cooking time 4–5 hours

Ingredients
2 cups dry red wine
1½ cups water
Zest and juice from 1 lemon
1 cup superfine sugar
2 cinnamon sticks
2 vanilla beans, split lengthwise
6 ripe pears, with stems

Directions
1. Combine all liquid ingredients and add them to the slow cooker.
2. Scrape the seeds of the vanilla beans into the slow cooker and stir gently.
3. Place the vanilla beans into the slow cooker.
4. Add the cinnamon sticks to the slow cooker.
5. Gently place the pears into the slow cooker. Try to cover the pears with the wine mixture.
6. Cook on high for 4–5 hours or until the pears are soft.
7. Serve with wine sauce drizzled over the top.

Nutrition (per serving)
Calories 202, fat 1 g, carbs 47.9 g,
protein 0.5 g, sodium 470 mg

Caramel Flan

This healthy dessert is so good you won't even miss the ice cream. The sweetness of the bananas, the crunch of the almonds and the creaminess of the yogurt erupt in your mouth for a flavor explosion.

Serves 5 | Prep. time 15 minutes | Cook time 2 hours and 15 minutes

Ingredients
1 (14-ounce) can sweetened condensed milk
14 ounces 2% or whole milk (measured in above can)
3 large eggs

Caramel Sauce
5 tablespoons (about half of a 12¼-ounce jar of caramel topping)
5 6-ounce ramekins

Whipped Cream, for serving

Directions
1. Whisk the condensed milk together with the whole milk and eggs.
2. Place 1 tablespoon of caramel sauce into each ramekin and swirl to coat the inside.
3. Fill the ramekins with the milk not quite to the top.
4. Add about an inch of water to the slow cooker and place the ramekins carefully inside.
5. Cook on high for 2 hours.
6. Remove the ramekins when the flan is set and let them cool completely.
7. To remove flan, run a knife carefully around the sides, then flip the flan onto a serving plate. Serve with whipped cream.

Nutrition (per serving)
Calories 249, fat 1.5 g, carbs 54.8 g,
protein 4.9 g, sodium 70 mg

Tiramisu Bread Pudding

This take on two classics is an excellent choice for the slow cooker. The espresso and Kahlua give it that wonderful coffee taste and aroma.

Serves 6 | Prep. time 30 minutes | Cooking time 2 hours

Ingredients
Bread Pudding
½ cup water
½ cup granulated sugar
1 tablespoon espresso powder
2 tablespoons Kahlua
1½ cups whole milk
½ cup heavy cream
5 large eggs
8 cups cubed (1-inch pieces) French bread

Topping
½ cup heavy cream
⅓ cup mascarpone cheese
1 tablespoon granulated sugar
1 teaspoon vanilla extract
Unsweetened cocoa, for dusting

Directions
1. Spray the slow cooker with nonstick cooking spray.
2. In a saucepan, mix together the water, sugar and espresso powder. Bring to boil and stir until the espresso has completely dissolved. Remove from the heat, stir in the Kahlua, and set aside.
3. In a mixing bowl, combine the eggs, milk, and cream, stirring until the eggs are completely incorporated. Pour in the cooled Kahlua mixture.

4. Take the cubed French bread and stir it into the milk mixture, pushing the bread down and stirring until all the bread cubes have been covered.
5. Transfer to the slow cooker and cook on low for 2 hours or until the pudding has set.
6. Make the topping by beating together the cream, mascarpone, sugar, and vanilla. Mix until fluffy and thick.
7. Serve a scoop of bread pudding with a dollop of topping. Enjoy!

Nutrition (per serving)
Calories 291, fat 19.4 g, carbs 24.3 g,
protein 4.6 g, sodium 31 mg

Cranberry Walnut Stuffed Apples

These delicious fruit-and-nut stuffed apples are an easy dessert that is perfect for fall. They plate beautifully, too, making them a wonderful treat for guests.

Serves 4–6 | Prep. time 10 minutes | Cooking time 4 hours

Ingredients
¾ cup walnuts, toasted and chopped
½ cup dried cranberries, chopped
⅓ cup packed light brown sugar
⅓ cup rolled oats
3 tablespoons unsalted butter, diced
1 tablespoon fresh lemon juice
½ teaspoon ground cinnamon
Kosher salt
4 large or 6 medium firm baking apples (such as Rome, Golden Delicious or Honey Crisp)
1 cup apple cider
Vanilla ice cream and pure maple syrup, for serving

Directions
1. In a small mixing bowl, combine the walnuts, cranberries, brown sugar, oats, butter, lemon juice, cinnamon, and salt.
2. Using your clean hands, mush the ingredients together until well combined.
3. Core the apples, being sure to leave the bottoms and sides intact.
4. Stuff the apples with the nut mixture and place them in the slow cooker. Pour apple cider over all the apples.

5. Cook on low for 4–5 hours or until the apples are soft. The time may vary depending on the size of your apples.
6. Serve with a scoop of ice cream and or maple syrup if desired.

Nutrition (per serving)
Calories 177, fat 5.6 g, carbs 33.6 g,
protein 2.8 g, sodium 50 mg

Recipe Index

Breakfast Recipes _____ 13
   Egg and Vegetable Breakfast Casserole _____ 13
   Breakfast Stuffed Peppers _____ 15
   Slow Cooker Frittata _____ 16
   Cranberry Apple Oatmeal _____ 17
   Blueberry Banana Steel Cut Oats _____ 18
   Berry Breakfast Quinoa _____ 19
Chicken and Poultry _____ 21
   Slow Cooker Greek Chicken _____ 21
   Chicken Gyros _____ 23
   Slow Cooker Chicken Cassoulet _____ 25
   Slow Cooker Chicken Provencal _____ 26
   Greek Style Turkey Roast _____ 27
   Garlic Chicken with Couscous _____ 28
   Chicken Karahi _____ 29
   Chicken Cacciatore with Orzo _____ 31
Beef and Veal Recipes _____ 33
   Tuscan Beef Stew _____ 33
   Cabbage Roll Casserole with Veal _____ 34
   Mediterranean Beef Stew _____ 35
   Slow Cooked Daube Provencal _____ 37
   Osso Bucco _____ 39
   Slow Cooker Beef Bourguignon _____ 41
   Balsamic Beef _____ 43
   Veal Pot Roast _____ 45
Pork and Lamb Recipes _____ 47
   Mediterranean Rice and Sausage _____ 47
   Lamb Shanks with Red Wine _____ 48
   Spanish Meatballs _____ 49
   Leg of Lamb with Rosemary and Garlic _____ 51
   Lemon Honey Lamb Shoulder _____ 52
   Italian Shredded Pork Stew _____ 53

Parmesan Honey Pork Loin Roast _____ 54
Braised Pork Loin with Port and Dried Plums _____ 55
Fish and Seafood Recipes _____ 57
   Seafood Cioppino _____ 57
   Shrimp Scampi _____ 59
   Tilapia Pesto _____ 60
   Seafood Stew_____ 61
   Lemon Dill Salmon _____ 62
   Seafood Paella_____ 63
Vegetarian Recipes_____ 65
   Turkish Stuffed Eggplant _____ 65
   Greek Rice _____ 67
   Slow Cooker Ratatouille _____ 69
   Chickpea Curry _____ 70
   Eggplant Parmigiana_____ 71
   Slow Cooked Caponata_____ 73
Soups_____ 75
   Minestrone Soup _____ 75
   Tuscan Cannellini Bean Soup _____ 77
   Moroccan Lentil Soup_____ 79
   Italian Meatball Soup_____ 80
Desserts_____ 81
   Cherry Clafoutis _____ 81
   Brown Rice Pudding _____ 82
   Poached Pears in Red Wine _____ 83
   Caramel Flan _____ 84
   Tiramisu Bread Pudding_____ 85
   Cranberry Walnut Stuffed Apples _____ 87

Also by Madison Miller

Here are some of Madison Miller's other cookbooks.

VEGAN SMOOTHIES
Nutritious Plant-Based Smoothie Recipes for Detox, Energy, and Weight Loss

Madison Miller

VEGAN COMFORT FOOD
Favorite Wholesome Plant-Based Recipes

Madison Miller

VEGAN INSTANT POT
Quick and Easy Plant-Based Vegan Recipes

Madison Miller

VEGAN SLOW COOKER
Healthy Plant-Based Vegan Crock Pot Recipes

Madison Miller

VEGAN 5-INGREDIENT
Quick and Easy Plant-Based Vegan Recipes

Madison Miller

VEGAN DESSERTS
Healthy and Sweet Plant-Based Recipes

Madison Miller

NO FLOUR NO SUGAR COOKBOOK
Quick and Easy Clean Eating Recipes for Weight Loss and a Healthier You

MADISON MILLER

NO FLOUR NO SUGAR COOKBOOK VOL.2
More Quick and Easy Clean Eating Recipes for Weight Loss and a Healthier You

MADISON MILLER

Cooking Conversion Charts

1. Measuring Equivalent Chart

Type	Imperial	Imperial	Metric
Weight	1 dry ounce		28g
	1 pound	16 dry ounces	0.45 kg
Volume	1 teaspoon		5 ml
	1 dessert spoon	2 teaspoons	10 ml
	1 tablespoon	3 teaspoons	15 ml
	1 Australian tablespoon	4 teaspoons	20 ml
	1 fluid ounce	2 tablespoons	30 ml
	1 cup	16 tablespoons	240 ml
	1 cup	8 fluid ounces	240 ml
	1 pint	2 cups	470 ml
	1 quart	2 pints	0.95 l
	1 gallon	4 quarts	3.8 l
Length	1 inch		2.54 cm

* Numbers are rounded to the closest equivalent

2. Oven Temperature Equivalent Chart

Fahrenheit (°F)	Celsius (°C)	Gas Mark
220	100	
225	110	1/4
250	120	1/2
275	140	1
300	150	2
325	160	3
350	180	4
375	190	5
400	200	6
425	220	7
450	230	8
475	250	9
500	260	

*   Celsius (°C) = T (°F)-32] * 5/9
** Fahrenheit (°F) = T (°C) * 9/5 + 32
*** Numbers are rounded to the closest equivalent

Printed in Great Britain
by Amazon